Rhymes Littl

Beverley Randell and Debbie Croft

Rhymes About Harry and Jet
Jet, the Little Robot	2
Jet Helps Harry	4

Rhymes About Sam and Bingo
Sam's Balloon Dog	6
Look Out for Bingo!	8
Bingo Goes to School	10

Rhymes About Josh and Lily
Lily's Apple	12
Josh's Shop	14
The Snow Bus	16

Jet, the Little Robot

This is my new toy.

Jet, the Robot, is his name.

When he waves and winks at me,

He wants to play a game.

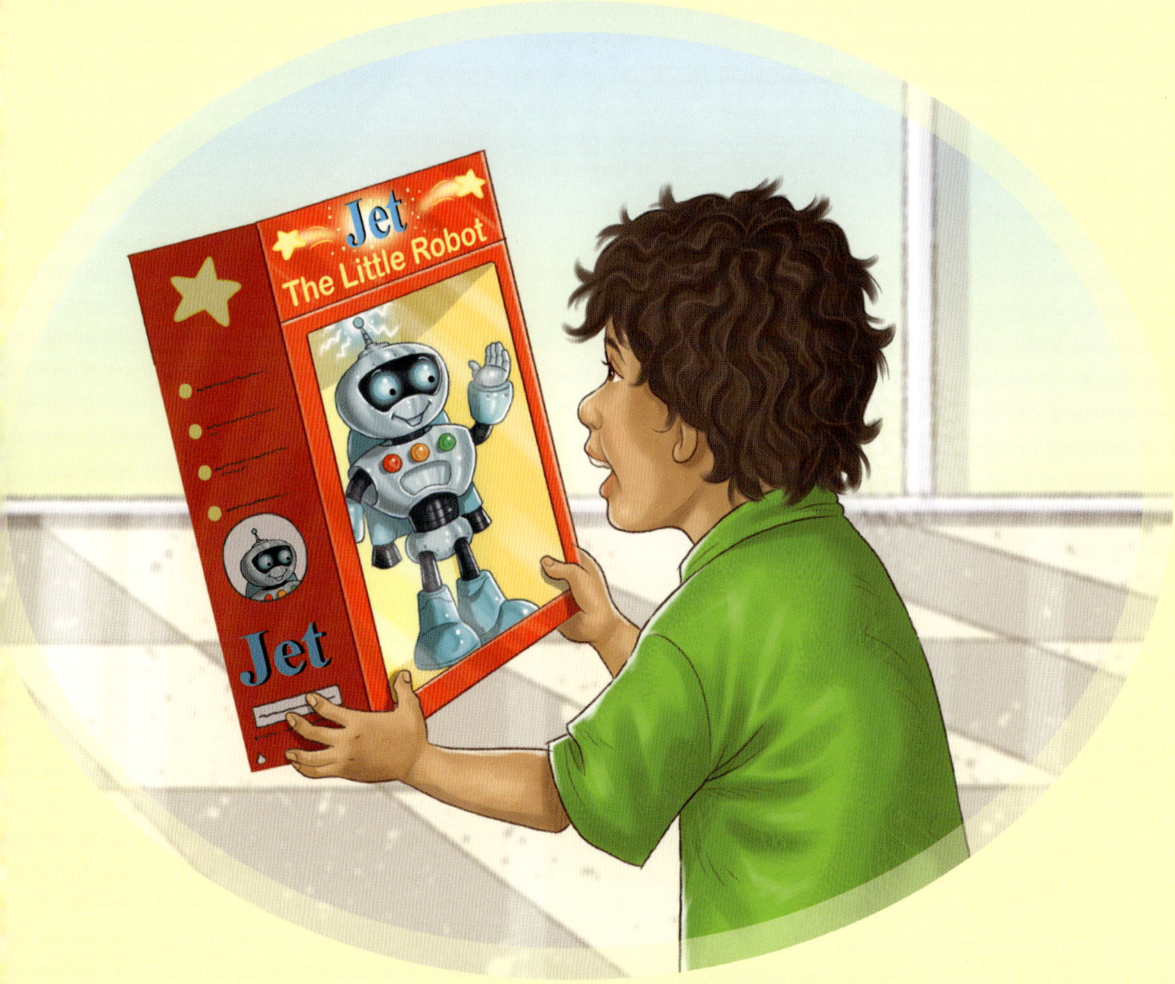
Jet
The Little Robot
Jet

Jet Helps Harry

Harry's room is messy.

He can't go out to play.

Jet, the Robot, helps him

Put all the things away!

5

Sam's Balloon Dog

The clown blew up a long balloon,
And then he made a knot.
He made a head — a tail —
and legs!
Sam loved that dog a lot.

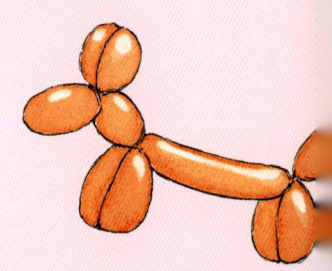

7

Look Out for Bingo!

Sam said, "Bingo, you are dripping. Stay outside. Yes, **out** you get!"
But Bingo shook his head and tail,
Making Sam as wet as wet!

9

Bingo Goes to School

When Bingo went to school

with Sam,

He did as he was told.

Sam told him, "**Stay!**

Stay, Bingo, **stay!**"

And he was good as gold.

11

Lily's Apple

Josh and Lily saw some ants,
Out in the garden one day.
The ants ate Lily's apple,
And did not run away.

13

Josh's Shop

"I do not have bananas.

There's no bread or eggs today.

But I do have two big ice creams.

We can eat them as we play."

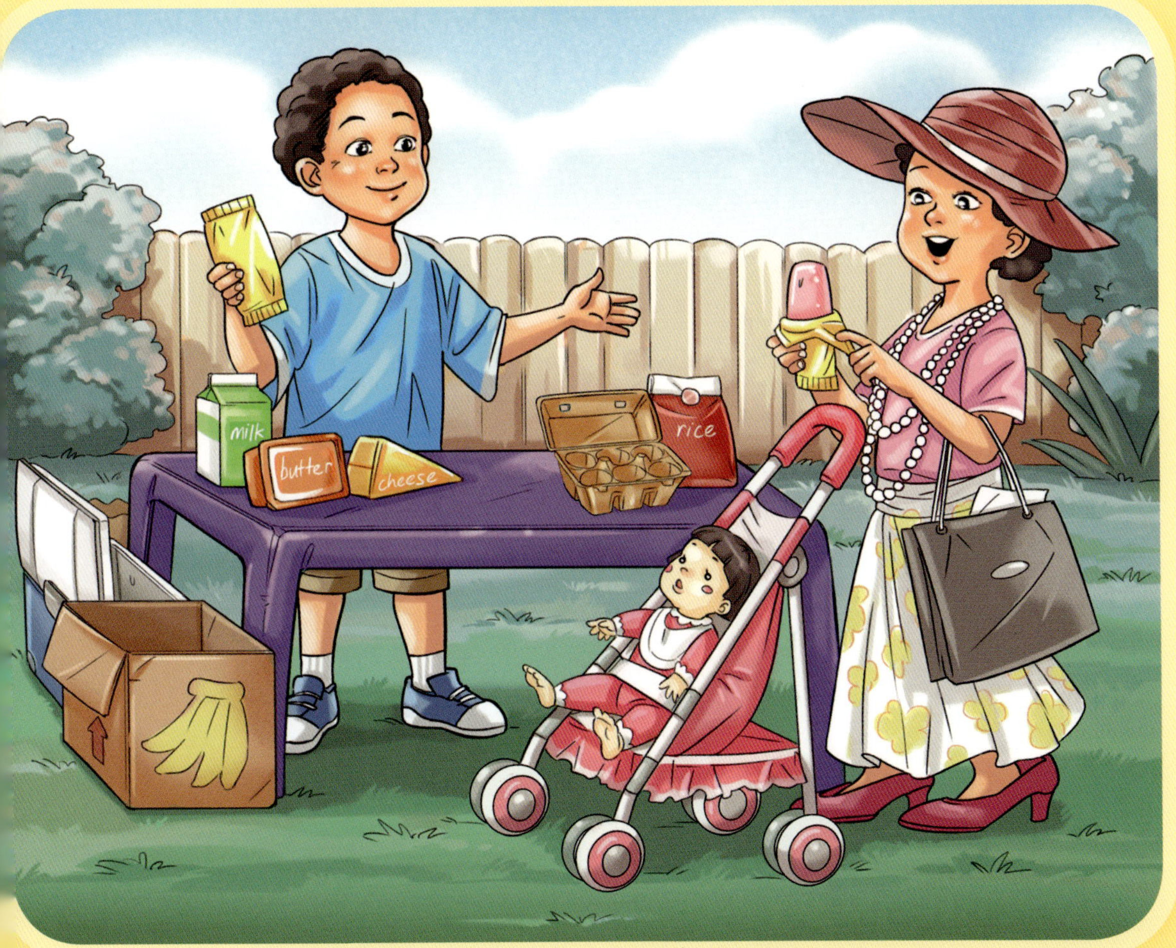
milk
butter
cheese
rice

The Snow Bus

Josh and Lily and Grandpa
Played with a bus in the snow.
"I will go first," shouted Lily.
"Look out!" she said. "Here I go!"